# LIVING
# AMONG
# THE GREAT
# PRETENDERS

# LIVING AMONG THE GREAT PRETENDERS

by Chuck Lightfoot

BearManor Media

2018

*Living Among the Great Pretenders*

© 2018  Chuck Lightfoot

All rights reserved.

Published in the United States of America by:

Bear Manor Media
P. O. Box 71426
Albany, GA 31708

bearmanormedia.com

Typesetting and layout by John Teehan

ISBN—978-1-62933-362-5

# Preface

*"If you are lucky enough to have lived in Paris as a young man, then wherever you go for the rest of your life it stays with you, for Paris is a moveable feast."*

Whom among us has not experienced a special place in time as did Ernest Hemmingway of Paris in the nineteen-twenties? Think about it. What is your special time and place? Everyone surely has one. The more I thought about my special place in time, I decided Santa Barbara, California in the nineteen-nineties.

# A Paradise For Great Pretenders

This charming southern California city shares the striking Pacific coastline with the looming Santa Ynez Mountains. Its Mediterranean climate, sunny beaches, Spanish-style architecture, flourishing culture, and laid-back lifestyle are major appeals of this captivating city. Tourists go to Hollywood to see the stars. The stars go to Santa Barbara as tourists, and many end up buying houses in Santa Barbara, preferably Montecito, a small unincorporated upscale community bordering Santa Barbara.

Montecito contains a superabundance of resident celebrities, film executives, and actors. Such a large concentration of celebs is rarely found within such a small piece of real estate. Film and TV actors regularly patronized the Montecito Café, the community's social hub in the nineties. (What its many patrons in the 90s called Montecito Café is now called Pierre Lafonde Market and Deli). Yes, I've indulged in my share of drinking the wines of Bordeaux and Burgundy at cafes along the Boulevards of Paris, but in comparison to outdoor people watching, they can't compete with the large cast of thespians that frequented this uniquely entertaining café in the nineteen-nineties.

On any random morning at Montecito Café in the nineties, you would likely see a variety of Santa Barbara's famous residents coming and going or seated at the outdoor tables along the wide sidewalk. Just imagine, if you will, that the entire cast of resident and visiting actors in the nineties make an appearance at Montecito Café—all in the same morning. With this in mind, enjoy this imaginary celeb-watching parade…

Along the walkway arrives Jane Seymour, star of many movies and the television series *Doctor Quinn, Medicine Woman*. Jane Seymour readily admits to being a pretender. "I have a lot of people inside me," Jane says, "and I am so blessed to be in a profession where people pay me to discover these people." As Jane Seymour walks along the runway she passes Christopher Lloyd, the actor of *Taxi* and *Back to the Future* fame. Seated tete-a-tete at the table with Lloyd is a lady who writes on a pad. Imagine Christopher Lloyd, a prolific writer, dictating another humorous episode of a popular sitcom.

Following Jane Seymour is the greatest of all the pretenders, Jonathan Winters, the chameleon actor who doesn't need to pretend. Jonathan *is* every character he portrays. As Jonathan strolls slowly along the row of tables firing off comic improves and adlibs, he enters the cafe leaving a wake of laughter. And once inside, he creates more smiles and chuckles.

Along comes another comic actor, Steve Martin, the wild and crazy guy who keeps a weekend retreat-home in Santa Barbara. Steve pauses at a table to converse with Montecito resident Julia Child. Imagine the gastronomic giant (she's six-foot-two-inches tall) giving Steve her latest recipe, chortling, "You can never add too much butter." Seated at a table next to them is Montecito frequenter, Chris Carter. The creator of the television series *The X-Files* is holding court with a flock of sci-fi fans, and judging by the spirited interaction, Carter seems to be thoroughly enjoying himself.

Check out who's advancing along the runway now. Robert Mitchum and Stuart Whitman, both of whom live a walking distance up San Ysidro Road from the café. These two popular actors are followed by Hollywood sex symbol Jane Russell and her friend Dorothy Mitchum. Next, Montecito's new resident arrives, this week's talk of the town, the multi-talented Geena Davis, fashion model, actress, writer, and athlete. Geena fits in harmoniously with Montecito's casual style of no pretense. Along comes Meg Ryan, pacing in long, rapid strides heading straight for that first cup of coffee. Even at her rapid pace it's hard to look at Meg without visualizing her seated in a restaurant faking an orgasm across from Billy Cristal in the rom-com *When Harry Met Sally*.

An SUV pulls into the parking lot and parks in view of the tables. There's something out of place here. All the vehicles in the lot are spiffy clean except the newly arrived SUV, which has mud-splattered wheels and dirt-streaked fenders. The driver's door opens, and out swings a long leg sporting a scuffed cowboy boot. The big, raw-boned man exits the vehicle and strides toward us. Jack Palance, Oscar winner for supporting actor in the film *City Slickers*, approaches our table. He greets us with a nod and taps a scuffed boot on the leg of an empty chair.

"Is this one mine?" he asks in a calm, low voice.

I answer, "We've been saving it for you, Jack."

He shows a grin and saunters into the café. Jack returns holding a large coffee and parks his hulking six-foot-four-inch frame onto the chair and joins in with us like we're old friends. When conversation gets around to talking about his Oscar, I asked him, "When you were up there on the stage during the awards presentation you dropped down and did several one-arm pushups. Quite a feat."

"Yeah," he said. "I get a lot about that. Everybody was standing around up there yacking, and I'm looking around wondering what to do, so I just did it."

"Well," I said, "your solo performance certainly turned out to be the most talked about act of the whole event."

Again, Jack shows a wide grin of a truly authentic guy who is also a writer, poet, painter, and owns and works his own horse and cattle ranch in nearby Ojai Valley. He finishes off his coffee and, with a friendly back wave and a "see you around," Jack strides to his authentic soil-smudged working vehicle and drives away.

Our attention is then drawn to Richard Widmark. He is guiding his feeble wife, Jean, by the elbow as she cautiously steps to an empty table. He arranges a chair and carefully helps her to be comfortably seated. With an affectionate touch on her shoulder, Richard walks into the Café and returns with coffees and croissants. To-and-fro he acknowledges no one other than with a polite nod. Not that Richard is anti-social. On the contrary, he is borderline deaf and avoids awkwardness because of his hearing impediment. It's hard to connect this real-life gentle person with his film character, Tommy Udo, who cackles wildly as he shoves the wheelchair-bound old woman down a flight of stairs in the 1947 film *Kiss of Death*.

A stream of pretenders quickly pass by in a rush for that first cup of coffee: John Ireland and Chris Mitchum, the boyishly handsome Rob Lowe, and the bodacious bombshell, Bo Derek. And yes, she is a ten!

Another pretender emerges in the background, Michael Douglas. His words, "With acting, you can be a child. Acting is wonderful for its innocence and fun." Michael strolls arm-in-arm with the sultry, sophisticated Welsh actress Catherine Zeta-Jones. By chance the couple run into Sharon Stone, one of the hottest pieces of property on the cinematic scene. An awkward encounter, perhaps? It's not uncommon for co-stars to have affairs, and Douglas and Stone co-starred in the film *Basic Instinct*. In that crime film, Michael plays a detective that interrogates Sharon's character suspected of being a killer. In this scene, Sharon, wearing a short skirt, uncrosses and slowly re-crosses her shapely legs, seductively revealing that she's not wearing underwear. (In show biz this is called the money shot.)

Evidently, the chance meeting of the threesome seems to be going well, probably because they're discussing Sharon's interest in feng shui. Sharon engaged Montecito guru Shawne Mitchell to counsel her on this ancient science to explore the ways energy interacts between her and her surroundings in order to rearrange things in her environment to nurture her lifestyle and purpose. Feng shui fits ideally into Californians unquenchable search for ancient oriental methods as solutions to perceived modern conundrums. As the genial threesome breaks up, along comes Montecito resident Karl Malden. Karl greets Michael as the son he never had, and Michael responds with affection to his mentor. Their professional and personal relationships solidified into a lasting friendship while co-starring in the 1970s television series *The Streets of San Francisco*. These two celebrated actors, as had so many other actors, chose Santa Barbara-Montecito as their favorite place in the nineties.

As did I. But, as the author Thomas Wolfe reminds us, "You can't go home again. Neither you, nor your favorite place, would be the same as your remembrances of it." But I say, Wolfe's view does not dissuade one from revisiting his favorite place in time through memory—and in print.

# A Special Place In Time

They called themselves Big John and Bad Jane, and little did we know when we moved next door to these two bigger-than-life characters how much they would affect our lives. Relocating to California from Georgia, my French-nationalized-American wife, Sylvie, and I observed that aspiring actors migrate to Los Angeles in search of stardom, and that many of the film stars migrate to Santa Barbara seeking a more halcyon lifestyle. It is into this paradise city where we settled into the house I inherited in 1990.

I knew from my late parents that a couple named John and Jane Peoples had bought the house next to theirs from the world-acclaimed artist Julien Ritter, and that Jane Peoples was a former movie actress. Beyond that, my parents, both in their nineties, knew little else about the couple next door.

While Sylvie remodeled the interior of the house I cut a pathway to the creek that flowed through our property. Whacking bushes with a machete close to the neighbor's fence, a gruff voice startled me.

"Hey, what ya doin' there?"

I looked up to see a large, goateed man across the fence watching me. He stood well over six feet tall in black cowboy boots, wearing black pants and a black shirt. I explained that my wife and I were new owners and I was making a foot path to the creek. He sized me up, grumbled "Oh," and ambled away.

When I reported this odd encounter to my wife, Sylvie worried that I may have alienated our new neighbor and hurried next door to repair any social damage I may have caused. When Sylvie came back she told me what had happened.

"When I knocked on the neighbor's door, a tall, attractive woman in a green jogging outfit appeared at the threshold. I introduced myself as her new neighbor. I told her, pardon me for staring but I feel that I know you from somewhere."

"'It happens a lot, honey,' she said. 'Probably from the movies.'"

"Yes! You are…Jane Russell."

"'I used to be. That gal on the screen was just an illusion.'" She spread her arms. 'This, honey, is the real Jane.'"

"The thought of having this gracious, self-deprecating neighbor stirred me to ask, 'Will you and your husband please join us for lunch tomorrow, or some other day, perhaps, whatever is convenient with you, of course, or…'"

"'Sure, honey,' She interrupted, smiling, saving me from further babel. 'We'd be delighted to have lunch with you tomorrow.'"

"Wow, I thought, her rapid response without consulting her husband showed who was in charge of this household. With an amused look she studied me and said, 'Frenchie, the Lord only knows what draws certain people together, and I have a feeling that you and I are going to have a wonderful friendship.'"

"Startled and happy, I quickly replied, 'Oh, me too, miss Russell!'"

"She held my hands. 'Friends call us Big John and Bad Jane.'"

"Oh, miss…er, Jane, I could never imagine you as being bad."

"Our new neighbor, the iconic film star Jane Russell said to me, 'Honey, you have no idea.'"

# The Friendship Lunch

For the Invitational lunch with our new neighbors. John and Jane Peoples, my wife prepared a bouillabaisse. Jane thought the fresh fish stew was "Gorgeous!" Using an adjective Sylvie hadn't heard to describe food, but spoken by the famous Hollywood star, the compliment was readily accepted and included thereafter. While our wives discussed food, John turned to me and without any mention of our first awkward encounter at the creek, invited me to lunch the following day with a buddy of his.

Stuart Whitman was a film and television actor whom I recognized from the movie *Those Wonderful Men in Their Flying Machines*, which I saw dubbed in French in Casablanca, Morocco at the Lynx Cinema. Stuart, John, and I got along well together, which developed into regular threesome boys-only luncheons. We began comparing different restaurants. In time, impressed by the food and the management, we chose as "our" restaurant, Café del Sol, situated at Santa Barbara's landmark bird refuge. Our nucleus group of three gradually doubled, then tripled. The owner, Jack Spears, was an accommodating restaurateur who became a friend. Rather than ordering from the wine list we paid a small corkage fee for the bottles we brought. Eventually Jack eliminated the corkage fee in appreciation of our burgeoning group of active regulars.

# The Road Trip

One Sunny morning the three of us were enjoying coffee at Montecito Café when John said that Jane wanted some pots for their patio. Stuart said he could use some pots for his ranch house. I said, "Sylvie can always use pots." John and Stuart chimed, "Mexico!"

The following day we rented a covered trailer and hooked it up to John's Mercedes and we headed south. John, being from Nacogdoches, Texas, knew all about Mexicans. "As we approached the border, John said with authority, "Speak only English, and pretend you don't understand Spanish."

At the border crossing to enter Mexico the guard raised an arm to stop us. He asked in Spanish what we had in the trailer. None of us spoke. The guard became frustrated, irritated. Finally, since I spoke Spanish having lived two years in Mexico, I said respectfully, "Esta vacio, señor. Nada adentro." The guard stepped back with a nod and waved us through.

While driving away inside Mexico, Stuart asked me, "What did you say to him back there?" "I told the guard, 'The trailer's empty, sir. Nothing's inside.'" Stuart grinned. From the back seat we could hear John's silence.

We drove through the congested border city of Tijuana down the Pacific Coast of Baja to the tourist town of Rosarito Beach, where we stopped at the first cantina for a taste of Mexico. Inside, we sat at a table and ordered Dos Equis beers and chicken and beef tacos. Stuart asked the barman, "Where can a fella get some pots around here?"

Startled, the barman stuttered nervously, "No, señor, we don't know nothin' about pot here."

I supressed a smile and said, "My amigo is not asking about pot, marijuana. He wants to know where we can buy big pots, potes grandes para flores. You know. Big flower pots."

The barman relaxed, relieved to know that we were not narcotics agents looking for extortion money or a quick bust. He gave us directions.

On the southern edge of town we shopped around, haggling over prices at several stores. When we struck the best deal for each of us, we began loading the trailer. John took charge, because in the military he had learned the correct order of size, weight, and displacement of cargo to attain optimum balance. After paying the grateful proprietor, we loaded our pots under John's learned direction: Stuart's pots first, mine second, and John's last, which both Stuart and I noted meant John's pots would be offloaded first when we got back to our respective houses.

After driving north through a rough patch of bumpy road we entered Tijuana, where we found a parking spot near an outdoor café. We sat at a table and ordered beers from a curious waiter eyeballing Stuart. I watched the waiter enter the café and return with another waiter and the barman. The three of them stood at our table looking at Stuart. Finally, the waiter said to Stuart, "You are the Norte Americano cowboy in films." Another waiter said, "We know your films here, Vaquero, cowboy. Muy Famoso." The barman said, "I saw you on television. You were the sheriff…on many movies."

Stuart nodded. "Those were episodes of the TV series *Cimarron Strip*." Stuart turned their attention to John. "Speaking of movies, my amigo here, he is the husband of Jane Russell."

The barman said, "The Jane Russell? The Outlaw?" He grasped both hands on his pectorals. "Tetas bonitas. You are lucky man, señor."

I noted John's grimace as he clutched his fist under the table. I kneed him and whispered, "Don't forget, amigo. We're in Mexico." John put on a false grin for the barman and shrugged it off. What John didn't understand was that the Mexican had given John a macho compliment for being husband to such a well-endowed, famous movie star.

A small crowd began to gather around us, buzzing comments: "Hollywood actors. Cowboys. Jane Russell is coming. Tetas!" Three mariachis marched by, stopped, and elbowed their way to us and began playing and singing their signature songs for turistas, "La Cucaracha" and "Guadalajara," followed by a nonstop repertoire of other tunes. We tipped the musicians and they bought us drinks with our money. More people gathered, and more beers and tequila arrived from all sides of our table. Two motorcycle policeman revved engines, halted, and strutted over to see what all the commotion was about. They too joined into whatever it was that was going on here.

When the crowd finally began to disperse, we asked the cops if they could tell us the route to the frontier. They readily obliged by providing us a motorcycle escort. With flashing lights, they led us through a maze of city streets to the border road.

When we returned to Santa Barbara we went directly to John's house to offload his pots first, as John had so expertly directed. Jane came running out all excited to see which pots John had chosen for their patio. As we pulled open the trailer's rear door, broken pieces of pots spilled out onto the driveway. It turned out that most of John's pots were either broken or badly cracked, caused by a bad patch of potholes on the rough road leading into Tijuana. Further inspection showed that the remaining pots in the front section of the trailer, those destined for Stuart and me, were all intact. Jane looked sadly at the sorry mess of what was left of her much-anticipated pots, before tramping away and re-entering the house.

Neither Stuart nor I ever again brought up the subject of pots to our good friend John. Although admittedly, we did get in some private chuckles over Big John, the self-proclaimed master cargo-loader.

# Poolside Party

The poolside cookout party at John and Jane's residence was well underway when the tall man made his solo entrance, his reputation preceding him. Tough, macho, movie star, boxer, incorrigible womanizer, hard-drinking barroom-brawler, pot-smoking jailbird, and the list goes on depending on who's shooting the fireworks. As he sauntered toward the self-service beverage bar a voice rose above the crowd.

"Hey Mitch, how ya' doing?"

Heads turned as Robert Mitchum called back. "Worse," he shouted, pouring himself a tall glass of vodka, straight, no ice.

As the evening progressed, somehow I found myself seated next to him, speaking to Mitchum as though he knew me well. Well, I sure as hell knew Robert Mitchum from a number of films I couldn't even count from the more than sixty movies he played in leading rolls. By now he was well into his second or third tall glass of vodka—straight, no ice—chain-smoking between drinks, recounting a mystifying story about Southeast Asia which I inferred he was in some unclear way involved with an unnamed intelligence agency. Out of the corner of my eye I saw Jane holding a camera pointed at us. The camera clicked, and she stepped up to him and smiled at the two of us. "Bob, I see that you met our new neighbor."

He looked at me, nodded, and looked back to Jane. "You're looking very well, my dear." He stood and bussed her cheek. There they stood, both aged now, cozy close and holding hands, Jane Russell and Robert Mitchum, dubbed Holywood's two hottest stars in Howard Hughes' 1951 RKO film *His Kind of Woman*.

Later I learned that while Sylvie and Jane Russell were talking about family and husbands, Sylvie happened to mention my periodic foreign trips prior to our settling in Santa Barbara. This news, I deduced, must have innocently got sucked into the local gossip circuit, fueling the rumor that surely those obscure trips of mine were somehow related to international intrigue. This all occurred before I had self-published my nonfiction book because I couldn't find a publisher to take it on. "Too controversial," they'd say. "Too hot to handle." So I self-published it. My nonfiction book, *REACT: CIA Black Ops*, finally came out in 2003, which was soon picked up by The Lyons Press that published my nonfiction book as a work of fiction by Robin Moore (in big print) and Chuck Lightfoot (not so big print) in 2004, all of which convinced me that the book publishing business is as creatively imaginative as Mitchum when he recounted that mystifying tale suggesting that he had in some capacity been functioning as a spook for some undisclosed government agency. At any rate, during the 90s while residing in Santa Barbara, my path frequently crossed that of Robert Mitchum, which further aroused my interest about the celebrated actor.

# Anatomy of a Star

My curious nature spurred me to learn more about this complex, enigmatic character. And the best place to begin, I figured, was inside the movie business. I researched old newspapers, magazines, and books to glean what Robert Mitchum's former producers, directors, co-stars, and journalists had said about him.

There's one story about Mitch that really cracked me up. While on the film *Rachel and the Strangers*, his co-star Loretta Young, a devout Catholic, insisted on a curse box to penalize bad-mouthed actors on a set a dollar for saying 'hell,' two dollars for 'damn,' and three dollars for 'shit.' It was reported that Mitch spoke out in bemusement, "And what does Miss Young charge for a fuck?"

Many people recollected on their memories and thoughts of Mitchum.

Sydney Pollack, Director of *Yakuza*: "Mitchum would drink out of a water glass, no ice, sip it slowly all day. And he would never pass out or never get falling down drunk. He'd reach a certain level and talk all day—just tell the most incredible range of stories."

Burt Kennedy, director of *The Good Guys and the Bad Guys*: "Bob's amazing in that if you listen to him, he sounds like he's a little crazy, but he's not at all. He's one of the brightest guys I know."

Ali MacGraw, co-star in *The Winds of War*: "There's tremendous danger in Bob's face and physical presence. There's an unpredictability, there's a don't-mess-with-me—and you never, never know which part of that personality is going to surface."

Ava Gardner, co-star in *My Forbidden Past*: "If I could have gotten him into bed, I would have. I think that every girl who ever worked with Bob fell in love with him, and I was no exception."

David Lean, director of *Ryan's Daughter*: He is a master of stillness. Other actors act. Mitchum *is*. Mitchum can make almost any other actor look like a hole in the screen."

Vincente Minnelli, director of *Home from the Hill*: "Few actors I've worked with bring so much of themselves to a picture, and none do it with such total lack of affectation as Mitchum does."

Shirley MacLaine, co-star in *Two for the Seesaw*: "I found him to be a complex mystery, multifaceted, ironically witty, shy to the point of detachment, and incapable of expressing what he personally desired. I willingly fell into the role of saving him from himself."

Charles Laughton, director of *Night of the Hunter*: "Mitchum is a great talent. All of this tough talk is a blind, you know. He speaks beautifully—when he wants to.

Howard Hawks, director of *El Dorado*: "I told Mitchum, you know, you're the biggest fraud I ever met in my life. Mitchum grinned. 'Why?' Because you pretend you don't care a damn thing about a scene, and you're the hardest working so and so I've ever known. Mitchum grinned. 'Don't tell anybody.'"

Myrna Loy, co-star in *The Red Pony*: "Oh, yes, Bob clowned around, but when it came to actual working he was all business.

He is one of those artists that make it look easy, a fine actor and intriguing man with so many sides to him."

Deborah Kerr, co-star in four films with Mitchum including *Sundowners*: "Bob is someone who's quite extraordinary. He can take a page of script, run his eyes down it, and he knows it. He must have a photographic memory."

Frank Sinatra, co-star in *Not as a Stranger*: "Mitch has got a heart as sensitive as an open wound. He's had to develop that tough exterior to protect the vital spots—his mind and his heart."

These anecdotal insights about Mitchum are from his former directors and co-stars. The following are from journalists and critics.

Kay Proctor: "Latching onto Bob Mitchum is something like walking into a cage of circus lions; you never can be sure just what's going to happen… He's neither willful nor rebellious, he's just a nonconformist."

David Thomas: "For a big man, he is immensely agile, capable of unsmiling humor, menace, and stoicism."

Jim Trombetta: "In the booze and broads' sweeps, big Bob is a well-advertised second-to-none."

Cecil Smith: "Robert Mitchum's name is trouble. You can paraphrase the old Shakespeare's line—some men are born to trouble, some achieve trouble, and some have trouble thrust upon them. Mitch qualifies in each department."

Richard Gehman: "Mitchum is Hollywood's foremost apostle of outrageous ob-stre'perous-ness. After being commended by a female reporter for not cursing, Mitchum said to the lady, 'Goddamn, but I'll be a son of a bitch if it don't beat the hell out of me.'"

Thyra Winslow: "That's Mitchum. A curious mixture of naivete, sophistication, adventure, indiscretion, simplicity, modesty, conceit, exhibitionism, introversion, extraversion, understanding, and doubt. A complex, interesting, and amusing personality."

John Belton: "He's tough and vulnerable, cynical and senti-mental. Mitchum embodies many contradictory qualities. He remains an enigmatic anarchist."

Bob Thomas: "Mitchum remains Mitchum—unregenerate, non-apologetic, a rare and endangered species. A Mitchum interview is always wide-ranging, sometimes unintelligible, and often libelous."

One evening at John and Jane Russell People's house, John, Stuart, Mitchum, and I were seated at a table drinking and talking. I noticed Mitch's heavy-lidded eyes watching me as though he was waiting to make up his mind. With a glance at John and Stuart, and indicating me, Mitch said in a vodka-lubricated voice, "What's with this guy?" During what was for me an awkward and puzzling silence, while I'm thinking, what's with him for blurting such an out-of-context, inappropriate remark? But I'm the new boy on the block fomenting friendships, so I clammed up. The conversation resumed with Mitch's unanswered question hanging in the air. Later, alone with John, I asked him, "What the hell was that about with Mitch?" John said, "Hmmm, Mitchum, well, sometimes when he opens his mouth you'll never know what's gonna come out." Later I asked my fellow cigar-smoking, beer-drinking, card-playing tennis partner, Stuart Whitman, about Mitch's remark, and Stuart told me the following story to enlighten me about Mitch's occasional unusual behavior.

"While entertaining two visiting Israeli Nobel Laureates at my home, Mitch dropped in unannounced—as he often did after drinking and in want of camaraderie. I introduced him to the two distinguished guests, who were complimentary of his films. Mitchum asked, 'And what do you gentlemen do?' They explained humbly that they were the honored recipients of the Nobel Humanitarian Prize.

"'Oh,' Mitchum said in booze-tainted voice. 'A couple of Jews, huh? I don't believe the Holocaust happened like it happened.'

"The Nobel Laureates sat silently riveted to their chairs. I rose from my seat and said, 'Mitch, come on. Let's go. Follow me.'

"Mitchum growled, 'I just got here. I need a drink.'

"'Later. Come on now,' I said. I could see he was well into his cups and glued to the chair. I stepped outside and brought in a wheelbarrow. The professors watched with wondering eyes as I coaxed and pulled and lifted him into the wheelbarrow with his arms and legs draped awkwardly over the sides, and Mitch's voice rumbling, 'I don'-wanna-go.'

"Once I got his limp body positioned inside so it wouldn't fall out, I looked at the professors and shrugged an apology that they understood with sympathetic nods. It's a long haul to Mitch's house, and he was heavy cargo. I left him in the wheelbarrow mumbling incoherently outside his house door, and I returned to host my distinguished guests."

During a barbecue party hosted by John and Jane Russell Peoples, Sylvie and Mitchum sat onto chairs that had been splashed by pool water. Sylvie went to the pool house for a hair dryer, and Mitch followed. John went for a camera and took a photo of Sylvie using the hair dryer on the backside of Mitch's pants. Mitch then stepped out of the pool house and announced. "I just got a blow job!" Well, as the saying goes, the silence was deafening.

Sylvie emerged from the pool house and aimed the hair dryer menacingly at Mitch, as though it were a weapon. Everyone broke into raucous laughter—that is, all except Dorothy Mitchum and Sylvie Lightfoot, who shared looks of mutual disapproval of Mitch's bad-boy behavior.

Personally, I do know this much about Mitch: as for his womanizing, he never seduced a woman who made herself unavailable. Mitch says of his only-wife-ever, "After all these years, Dorothy knows what to expect and how to handle me. She's the best, and she knows more about the business than I do." And Jane Russell, who had co-starred in two of his films, and was also a Montecito neighbor and close friend of the Mitchum family, said, "With Robert Mitchum, it's Dorothy. They have a *family-family*—married to the same woman whom he loves and provided for their children and was always there to help them with their careers."

As for Mitchum's acting prowess, few would disagree with Dan Curtis, producer and director of *The Winds of War* and *War and Remembrance*: "He's the biggest pro in the world."

As for the scandalous, over-publicized jail time for a marijuana bust, Mitch did ask the photographers not to take pictures of him behind bars, because his kids might see them. Otherwise, he showed no discomfort. On the contrary, he actually joked, "My jail term was one of the happiest times of my life. Jail is like Palm Springs without the riffraff, only you meet a better class of people."

Janet Maslin of *The New York Times* observed, "There's something impressive about the imperturbability with which Robert Mitchum marches through the most potentially embarrassing situations."

Mitch and my paths crossed at various social events, always friendly, yet never friends in the true sense of that precious word. Mitch himself has said, "I don't have any really close men friends. I'm more or less a loner anyway." Along with many others who knew him, Mitch will remain like Winston Churchill's apt description of Russia: "A riddle wrapped up in a mystery inside an enigma."

When I last saw Mitch at his house with my pals John Peoples and Stuart Whitman, Mitch was wearing an oxygen apparatus while defiantly smoking a cigarette. John remarked that Mitch would ignite the thing and shoot off like a rocket into space. I asked Mitch about writing his memoirs. He blew smoke. "Why? I already told what I know to the Los Angeles Police Department."

It is said that the end of every journey is home. With Dorothy at his side in their Santa Barbara-Montecito home, Mitch died at the age of seventy-nine from lung cancer and emphysema on July 1, 1997.

# The Greatest of All Pretenders

Santa Barbara-Montecito resident and habitué of Montecito Café, the multi-talented actor-comedian-painter-writer was very well known around our community for being a prolific raconteur. At his daughter Lucinda's wedding in Montecito, his wife, Eileen, was nervous because Jonathan was absent. She caught the eye of Stuart Whitman, who was seated close to her. With a shrug, Eileen whispered "Where is Johnathan?" Stuart hand-signaled he'd go look for him. Stuart went outside and found Jonathan in the parking lot. The master of improve comedy stood surrounded by a group of admirers reveling in his rapid-fire routines. Stuart took him away by the elbow with an apology to the fans and guided him inside the church so that Jonathan Winters could give his anxious daughter away in marriage.

One morning, John Peoples and I were seated at Montecito Café, amusing ourselves over Stuart's story, when coincidentally, Johnathan marched by clad in an odd array of military garb. He hesitated before us, stiffened, and saluted.

"Marine Corporal Winters reporting for duty." He studied us. "Do I call you two gentlemen officers, sir?"

"Yes, corporal," I replied.

"You can call Lieutenant Colonel Peoples here, sir. I'm corporal Lightfoot."

Johnathan saluted John. "Of course. Hello, John. Please give Jane my regards." He turned to me. "Fellow corporal, huh? What branch?"

"Army," I said. "Fifth Regimental Combat Team."

"Combat, huh?"

"No," I said. "I missed actual combat by a few months. By the time I got to Korea the war had ended."

Johnathan's rubbery face squinted into a mosaic of folds. "Yes, I heard about that, Corporal. The enemy quit because they knew you were coming."

"Yeah," I said. "That's the way it happened."

Johnathan smiled, then said, "I served in the Pacific. In '45, during World War II." His cherub face reshaped into something serious, reflective. "I've always been proud of being a Marine. I won't hesitate to defend the Corps."

"Damn straight," I said.

"Sempre fi," John chimed.

Johnathan said, "Say, how'd you two veterans like to come up to my place and I'll show you around?"

John and I both readily agreed, wondering what to expect from the unpredictable connoisseur of humor and foibles. We had heard stories of Jonathan's penchant for collecting things, but nothing prepared us for what was to come.

Upon entering Jonathan's home, he waved his arm toward a table larger than a pool table. On it, tiny figures of soldiers were positioned as two opposing forces in battle formations. Jonathan said straight-faced, "They haven't moved in over a year. I'm still waiting to see which army will win." He motioned us to follow him into an adjoining room filled with all kinds of hats and caps, costumes and outfits, some of which he was known to wear strolling around the neighborhood. As I gazed about the unusual display, I became aware of standing on Jonathan's hallowed ground—his own world among the uniforms and costumes worn by characters he created. Observing us taking it all in, Jonathan said, "So many people not only enjoy, but truly love dressing up and pretending they're anybody but who they really are."

Leading us into another room, he said, "I feel sorry for people who don't have a hobby." Glancing around this room, Jonathan's hobby was displayed by his surrealistic paintings and ink etchings hung on the walls. "These are my fantasy paintings." He seemed most comfortable in this room among the art he had created. "I learned to observe people," he said, adding, "and life all around us, through art."

After completing the tour of his house, or that part of it he wished to show us, he invited us for drinks. He brought us a couple of beers and a soda for himself. "I don't drink alcohol," he said. "I was an alcoholic. It was killing me, so I gave it up." He snapped a thumb and finger. "Just like that, I quit. Haven't touched it since." He even spoke about his two nervous breakdowns and being hospitalized for treatment of bipolar disorder. He paused a moment and said, "I told you I was a Marine. A corporal, in the Pacific Theater." He paused, and as though a switch had flipped, Jonathan morphed into another person, a sad, rotund, child-like figure with a blank stare. "When I came home from the war," he said in a low voice, "I went to my room to reminisce and go through my old toys. But they weren't there. I asked my mother, 'what happened to my toys?' She answered, 'Why, dear, I gave them all to the children at the mission.' I said, 'They weren't for you to give away. You should have written me, because there were some things I had hoped to keep forever.' Mother said, 'But how did I know you would be coming home?'"

When Jonathan broke the silence, his voice took on a tone I hadn't heard before. "You know what really frightened me the most? Mom and Dad, 'cause they drink every night, and though they never beat me, they're always saying they never shoulda had me." His lips compressed. He swallowed. "Mom and Dad never understood me, and I didn't understand them." He seemed to ponder this, and then as though he had an epiphany, he said, "Because I forgot to grow up!" He frowned, and said in curious earnest, "Why did I forget to grow up?"

I often wondered if Jonathan ever found the answer to his sentient question. And thinking back about the surprising, insightfully interesting visit with such an unusual, complex man, whom I now considered a friend, I checked out his book from the Montecito Library. *Winters' Tales: Stories and Observations for the Unusual*, Jonathan inscribed, is a book for adults that appeals to the child in all of us.

*Brevity is the soul of wit*, Hamlet tells us, and Jonathan's brief stories, peppered with keen perceptions and cleaver, witty expressions, clearly reflect The Bard's proverb. Through the power of story, no matter how brief, Jonathan takes on the most mundane incidents of life. Some tales are sad yet humorous, and never lacking interest and thought-provoking, surprise endings. As Socrates tells us, *Wisdom begins in wonder*. Jonathan spent his entire life in a child-like wonderland. He told me that when he writes his autobiography, the book's title will be, *In Search of a Playground*. His curiosity, his comedy, his writing, his art, his whole body of work, his very life, all attest to the fact that Jonathan Winters is one very funny, wise, creative dude.

# The Dinner Party

The guest of honor for the dinner party would be Jonathan Winters. This gesture of neighborly reciprocity came about by Jonathan inviting me into his home to show his art work and collectibles. When Sylvie called to invite the Winters's to dinner, she asked Jonathan his food preference. He, knowing my wife was French, expressed his love of all French cuisine. He emphasized special interest in escargot and frog legs.

Sylvie began planning immediately. Ten persons could be seated comfortably at our patio table, so she invited three additional couples who were friends of both the Winters and ours: John and Jane Russell Peoples, Robert and Dorothy Mitchum, and Andy and Dolly Granatelli.

Then, Sylvie confronted the challenge to compose a menu in the classical French style, *A la Francaise*, which put her into a conundrum. "Escargot and frog legs together in the same meal! *Zut alors*!" she exclaimed.

But as my wife says when faced with such a quandary, "What woman wants, God wants." Thus, she solved the culinary puzzle by presenting escargot as hors d'oeuvres, followed by a soup.

"Make it a vichysoise," I chimed in.

Sylvie answered, "That's a bit too bland, don't you think?"

"What I think," I replied, "is how much fun Jonathan will have playing with that word. Think about it. *Veee-shee-swahzzuh*! He'll likely make a whole routine out of that one."

Sylvie conceded reluctantly, rather than harangue me about the proper order and balance to the palate of a classically orchestrated French meal. For seafood, which normally would be next in order, she put Jonathan's obligatory frog legs, a la provencale, of course, since Sylvie is connected to provence, a lime sorbet to cleanse the palate, followed by her *plat de resistance*, steak au poivre, done with filet mignon and freshly crushed black peppercorns, and French cognac. And, of course, like all French chefs, Sylvie never reveals at least one secret ingredient of her sauce. The pepper steak was accompanied by fresh baby carrots and baby green beans. Next, a mixed watercress and Boston lettuce salad with Sylvie's own dressing, followed by the only three French cheeses she was able to find locally: Boursin au poivre, Camembert, and Roquefort. And plentiful French bread, and a careful pairing of the French wines with each course. For desert, she made a crème brulèe, followed by fresh fruits, coffee, and assorted liqueurs. Voila!

The guests arrived under a soft summer evening to the enchanting tones of nearby Toro Canyon Creek. We sipped aperitifs, and with appetites stimulated, the serving began. This carefully orchestrated French dinner, even allowing for the unconventional combining of escargot and frog legs in the same meal, which was otherwise meticulously planned and prepared by Chef Sylvie at Chez Lightfoot for our distinguished guests, gradually turned into something not planned.

After the guests finished eating, Jonathan pulled Sylvie aside to inquire if she had any remaining escargot. "Yes," Sylvie replied. "Shall I put them in, what do you call, a doggy bag?"

"But no, Madame," Jonathan said in exaggerated French-accented English. "May I take zee delicious escargot at zee present time, if it so pleases to you, madame."

Sylvie smiled. "As you wish, monsieur." She went inside and brought back several escargots, and a French beret, which she placed on his head at a rakish angle to his absolute delight. "Voila monsieur," Sylvie said. "Maintenant vous etes un Francais honoraire."

The former American Marine corporal rose from his seat and snapped to attention with a military salute. "As a Francais honoraire, I am now to be called Corporal Vee-shee-swahzuh." Sylvie laughed, and bussed both his chubby cheeks. He bowed and kissed her hand. "Corporal Vee-shee-swahzuh at your service, madame."

Sylvie turned her head to me, and I gave her a thumbs-up. Everyone laughed as Jonathan, the skilled vocalizer, continued voicing more of his unique, un-comprehensible French sounds. Robert Mitchum waved Sylvie to him. Frowning down at the wine and liqueur bottles, he asked Sylvie if she had any vodka or tequila. Sylvie readily obliged his request by bringing him a full bottle of each, along with a water glass without ice. He quickly filled the glass and began drinking and telling tales to anyone who pretended to listen to him. John and Jane Russell Peoples, both known at the time to drink anything with alcohol in it, drank contentedly from the colorful array of bottles of assorted liqueurs aligned before them. Andy Granatelli was pleasantly occupied consuming extra cuts of filet mignon, which Sylvie brought him, knowing by experience the hefty former racecar driver (Mister 500) and business tycoon would crave and enjoy even after a full meal.

I watched Sylvie standing back, observing the stage of performing actors—our neighbors, our friends. Dorothy, Jane, Dolly, and Eileen called out verbal accolades to Sylvie. Sylvie replied humbly, "Food does always taste better when shared with friends." Jonathan, now totally French and speaking French-sounding gibberish, created joyful laughter all about him. I could see the joy of being Jonathan Winters dance on his cherubic face. It struck me at that moment that Jonathan's greatest joy is not his hobby as artist and collector, as I surmised at his home. No, Jonathan's supreme joy is simply making people laugh. I caught Sylvie's eye from across the table of our guests, all well-satiated, happy and buckling in laughter over Corporal Vee-shee-swazuh's non-stop performance. Sylvie read my lips, "Thank you. I love you." She blew me a kiss, and I read her lips, "I love you too."

# My Loving Wife Sylvie

After living outside the U.S. for more than a decade, my wife Sylvie and I finally decided to settle in America. Because of the various countries we had lived in, we had mostly conversed in French or Spanish. Consequently, those first few years in the U.S. were difficult for her because of the language. Slowly, Sylvie began learning English, with several bumps along the way.

While reminiscing on shared experiences, the subject of awkward linguistic incidents that she had encountered in her new land came up. For example, that time when a lady in need of an alcoholic drink asked her, "Is this a dry county?" Sylvie replied, "Oh, no, madam, it often gets very humid here."

And the time in a department store when an overweight lady asked Sylvie where she could find yardage. Sylvie pointed to a door at the end of the long room. "On the other side of that door, madam." The heavy woman lumbered across the long room that led outside, into a yard. One can only imagine the lady huffing and puffing, angrily looking for Sylvie, who had already left the store, pleased that she had assisted the lady to find yardage.

And, that one about the middle-aged man who sidled up to Sylvie and panted in a whisper, "I'm horny." Sylvie regarded him with pity, because in Italian horny is cornuto, which she connected in French to cocu, which means a man whose wife is unfaithful. "Oh, I am so sorry, sir," Sylvie said in a soft, compassionate voice. "I'm sure your pain will pass, and that in time it will all work out between you and your wife." The man stood rigid, dumfounded, surely thinking this woman was a crazy person, and turned and hurried away not looking back.

And then there was that very confusing incident with the doctor. Sylvie's friend recommended a doctor, and she called his office for an appointment. Sylvie asked the receptionist to schedule a rendezvous with the doctor.

The receptionist replied hesitantly, "You want, a rendezvous with the doctor?"

"Yes. I've been told he is very good."

"One moment, please."

Another woman came on the line. Sylvie again asked for a rendezvous with the doctor. Sylvie heard giggles in the background.

Finally, the doctor came on the line. "This is Doctor Smith. May I help you?"

"Yes, doctor. I would like to make a rendezvous with you."

"You want a rendezvous with me? Do I know you?"

"No, sir. I've recently arrived here, and I've been told you are very good."

Well, this linguistic conundrum finally got sorted out and understood that what this French lady wanted was a doctors' appointment for a physical, which she finally got, causing much amusement to everyone in the doctor's office—especially Doctor Smith.

# Great Pretenders At the Stonehouse Restaurant

Since I first met Sylvie in Casablanca, Morocco, and through-out all the countries we traveled to and lived in for my work, Sylvie would seek some sort of employment to avoid boredom and satisfy her talents and her energy. Living in Santa Barbara was no exception. One late evening at our Florida home in my study, I asked my wife to please help me with some information about the highly acclaimed restaurant where she worked.

"What for?" Sylvie asked.

"It's for the book I'm writing. You know, about the two of us living among the great pretenders in Santa Barbara in the nineteen nineties."

"That is last century's news. You should be writing about living among the great retirees in Florida in the twenty-teens."

"C'mon, cheri. Please work with me on this."

"What do you want to know?"

"What you did there, at the Stonehouse Restaurant?"

"Did? I worked. *Bien sur.* Of course."

"Give me some examples. Think as though being back there at the restaurant in the nineties."

"What is this, a how-to manual of a restaurant manager?"

I waited patiently.

"Let me think," she said. "It's been over twenty years, you know. Okay. Let's see. As day manager I arrive early before the employees. I check if there are any messages from the night manager. I count the cash in the register, and I see what reservations we have for lunch. I get with Mark, the French chef, about any menu changes and specials and..."

"Whoa. Slow down. The book is about people. Patrons who are celebs, actors."

Sylvie enthusiastically raised an arm. "First I must tell you about the cuisine. It's the very best, of course. The owners hire only the best French chefs. Our chef, Mark, at the Stonehouse Restaurant, he is the very best! The menu is French, of course. The owners were French, you know. They also own the Auberge de Soleil, a very prestigious hotel in the vineyards of Napa Valley.

"Also, the very best?"

She gives me a look that I understand only too well. "*Tu te moques de moi?*"

"I do not mock you. Please continue. Celebrities. Any famous persons come to the Ranch and dine at the Stonehouse?"

"Yes. Winston Churchill is registered as having been a guest at the San Ysidro Ranch, and John and Jaqueline Kennedy stayed there during their honeymoon."

"Impressive. How about celebrities when you were there?"

"Hollywood types, actors, writers, most of them from Los Angeles. Weekends mostly. And, of course, we had our local celebrities."

"Any anecdotes, vignettes about them you recall?"

"Richard Widmark," Sylvie says. "He comes in several times a week. Only for breakfast. He sits at *his* corner table and reads the newspaper. Doesn't speak or acknowledge anybody. He's hard of hearing, you know. Without ordering, the waiter routinely brings him orange juice, oatmeal, and coffee, with one refill. It's always the same. He finishes and leaves a dollar tip on the table and walks out with his newspaper. Always the same."

"What else you got?

"Meg Ryan," Sylvie says. "When I told Mark, the chef, that Meg Ryan had made a reservation for lunch, he got all excited. He said, 'Meg Ryan. The beautiful actress is coming here, today? I have to meet her! I'll create a special dish and name it after her.'"

"Well, when Mark's dream actress arrived, I pointed her out to him. I watched him strut to her table. They spoke briefly as he hovered stiffly at the table. When Mark returned I could read his disappointment. 'I told you,' I said to him. 'Your wife is prettier.'"

"The Meg Ryan dish was never created," Sylvie told me. "When it comes to women, the French men can be very French, you know?" I nodded mechanically, and she continued. "On a similar subject, when word got out that Jamie Lee Curtis, you know, the daughter of actor Tony Curtis and actress Janet Leigh, was at the swimming pool wearing a bikini, several male employees raced to the pool in fits of hormonal fantasies. And, they too returned forlorn and disappointed with unfulfilled dreams." Sylvie pondered this. "When will the cinema audience learn that what you see on that big screen is just an illusion. That's what Jane Russell told me. Anyway, I must say, that in addition to their respective performance talents, both Ryan and Curtis being naturally photogenic did enhance their bigger-than-life screen appearances. Another thing positive about them is when one considers the heavy competition they had to surpass to get those choice acting gigs. That in itself is a great achievement."

"Here's another anecdote for you," Sylvie said. *Good*, I thought, *she's really on a roll now*. "It's about a television actor," she said. "While I was briefly standing in at the reception desk to cover for the regular girl, a man walked in. He had an issue with his room that was quickly resolved, and he turned to leave. He stepped toward the door, stopped and turned back. 'Do you know who I am?' he asked.

"'Yes,' I replied. 'You are registered here. You are Mister Danson.'

"He started to leave, and hesitated. 'Does that ring a bell to you, about who I am?'

"'If I recall correctly, sir, I think you were using a different name on that TV program, the one about a bar?'

"'*Cheers*,' he said.

"'Yes, *Cheers*,' I repeated.

"He stood looking at me, as though waiting for something to happen, then he turned, shaking his head, and stepped out the door. *How very strange*, I thought. When I told our neighbor John about the incident, John, the Hollywood expert, since he was married to Jane Russell, said, 'It's the actor's ego. No doubt Ted Danson wanted you to ask for an autograph, a picture, or just to be recognized and be in awe of his presence.'"

Sylvie told me about another odd incident. "It started," she said, "with a gentleman who was seated in the restaurant beside an attractive lady with long red hair. He called me to his table and asked if we had a mic. I went to the kitchen and asked if we had a Mike working for us. No one knew of a Mike, so I returned to the man and told him that we didn't have a Mike working here. He looked at me oddly and said, "I asked for a microphone."

"Oh, pardon, monsieur, I'll see." I walked away self-consciously, and no matter how hard the couple tried to stifle their laughter I could still hear them chuckling until the kitchen door closed behind me. I was told that the man was Stacy Keach, an actor also noted for his singing talent.

"Well, we didn't have a mic. That's it," Sylvie said. "That's the Stonehouse Restaurant. A long time ago." She reflected, "Yet, in some ways it seems just like yesterday." She stepped away with a back wave, saying, "Lots of luck, with that book of yours."

My dear wife of over fifty years left me pondering what she really meant by "Lots of luck with that book of yours." I do know this, that when it comes to critiquing, French people, especially French women, can be very French, you know?

Chuck and Mitchum

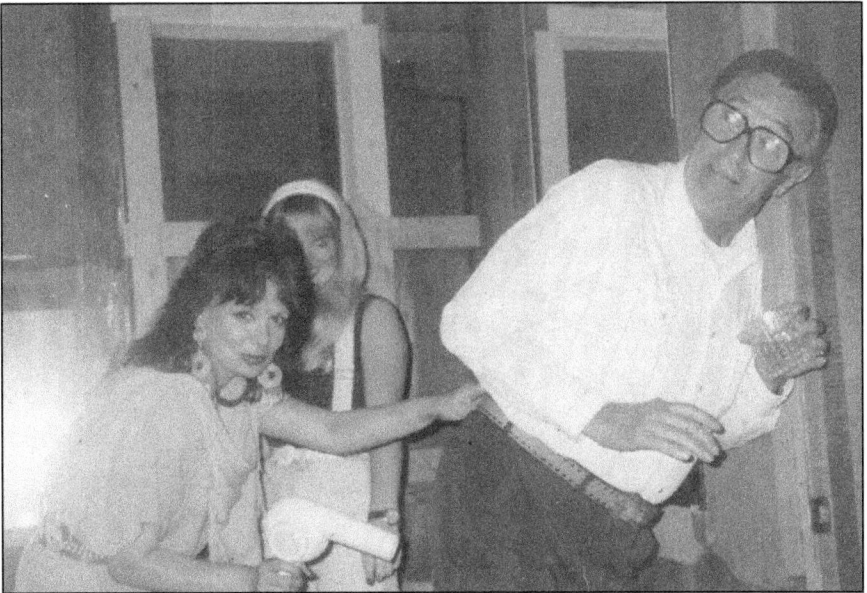

Sylvie and Mitchum (unidentified spy)

Sylvie and Mitchum

Jane Russell and Chuck

Jonathan Winters

Jonathan Winters and Chuck

Sylvie, Joyce Patterson and Stuart Whitman

John Peoples, Stuart Whitman and Chuck

Debbie Reynolds, Jane Russell and Sylvie

Eva Gabor and Sylvie

Jane Russell, June Allyson and Sylvie

Chuck and Stuart Whitman

Chuck, John Peoples, Richard Adams and Stuart Whitman,

Arlene Dahl and Chuck

Arlene Dahl and Chuck

Mark Rosen and Sylvie

Chuck and Bob Kane

Chuck, Bob Kane and Martha Smilgis

Robert Mitchum, Dolly Granetelli and Andy Granatelli
Standing: Babs Allen, Sylvie and John Peoples

Andy Granatelli and Sylvie

Syd Charisse, Chuck, Quintin Allan, Sylvie, John Peoples and Ann Miller in Las Vegas

Top row: Chuck, Jane Russell and husband John
The end of a southern California lunch

# Meeting New Friends

One quiet afternoon, seated at John Peoples's patio overlooking Toro Canyon Creek, we were discussing life, and out of the blue I said, "I want to learn Italian."

John gave me a where-did-that-come-from look. "Why?" he finally asked.

I said, "A good friend of mine, Marco Monachio, died, and I was thinking about something he had told me: 'There are two kinds of people in this world, Italians and those who want to be Italians.'"

Perhaps stimulated by the profundity of deceased Marco's remark, the next day John and I enrolled in an Italian class at the local adult education center. John, evidently having no personal affinity with Italians, quit after the first day, while I continued with a dozen other students, including Dolly Granatelli, wife of the famous race car driver and business tycoon Andy Granatelli.

One day Dolly invited the entire class to her house for lunch. She sat me next to her husband. As the lunch progressed, Andy, who is an Italian-American, asked me, "Why do you want to learn Italian?" I told him what my deceased friend Marco Monacho said about there being two kinds of people, Italians, and those who want to be Italians.

Andy smiled. "He's right, you know." I shared his smile. He said, "Dolly told me Jane Russells's husband quit the class. Do you know him?"

"Yeah. John is my neighbor and a friend."

Andy said, "Why don't you guys come over sometime and I'll show you my antique car collection."

John and I showed up with Stuart Whitman a couple days later for a prideful show directed by Mister 500 himself. The large, air-tight, temperature-controlled building housed over three dozen prized antique automobiles, all polished and in perfect condition displayed on a red carpet. After viewing several cars, Andy excused himself. "You fellows look around and stay as long as you like." Our large, heavyweight gracious host walked to the entrance door and sat heavily into a chair enjoying watching us enjoy his pride and joy classic automobiles.

A week or so later Sylvie and I were invited to a garden luncheon party at the Granatelli's estate that occupied a large quantity of acreage in the heart of Montecito. What Dolly Granatelli had modestly referred to her fellow students as her 'house' was a magnificent mansion surrounded by a tennis court, indoor pool, multimanicured gardens, a vegetable garden, and of course Andy's treasured classic automobile museum. Upon arrival, Sylvie separated to join Jane Russell, and I sat next to Ernest Borgnine. The actor and I hadn't met before, but we fell easily into conversation about movies. I asked him about the film *The Wild Bunch*, where he and several actors splashed around inside huge vats of wine with nude Mexican babes. He laughed. "It was crazy, you know. We had a lot of fun on that picture." He paused. "A lot of hard work too."

I wasn't at all sure he was talking about work or play. Anyway, when we were talking about the movie *From Here to Eternity*, I said, "That fight you had with Burt Lancaster was so real. How'd you two pull it off?"

He said, "Yeah that was a tough one. We had to do several takes, and…" He stopped abruptly, staring away, and said, "Pardon me. That woman in white there, I can't take my eyes off her."

I followed his look and called to the woman in white. "Sylvie, viens ici s'il te plait." As my stunning wife advanced, Ernest said, "And she's French too!" I made introductions, and after some charming small talk Sylvie apologized and pulled me away to join her and Jane Russell.

As much as I enjoyed my friendly tete-a-tete with Ernest Borgnine, my wife had a totally different experience with him. While I was on a business trip Sylvie got a telephone call from Andy Granatelli saying he is sending a car to pick her up to join several friends for lunch. When I returned from my trip she told me all about it.

Sylvie said, "When I entered the large room I spotted Andy and Dolly Granatelli with John and Jane Russell Peoples, and I was ushered to a chair toward the end of the left side of the U-shaped table. The persons seated across from me nodded politely, and the young man facing me, who had been conversing with a young, attractive blond lady seated next to him also turned his attention on me. Although feeling awkward, I feigned polite interest as he spoke of his passion for surfing and chasing the big waves in many countries.

"I glanced up on an impulse to recognize the bulky man approaching. Unlike our first encounter, Ernest Borgnine was not smiling now. He halted beside me, and with a hand on the back of my chair and the other hand planted on the table he leaned toward the talkative surfer. How odd, I thought. He was obviously upset, and I didn't know what to expect. Borgnine assailed the surfer with undisguised tones of contempt. 'What do you think you're here for?' He indicated the blond lady. 'She's just separated from her husband, and she is here from Texas and you're supposed to be her companion to show her around.' From my view I sensed the surfer cringe, probably I supposed, aching to be elsewhere from this harangue. Borgnine turned his head and glared at me. 'And you, why do you distract him!' I bit my tongue to avoid an irrational verbal battle. The surfer remained silent, watching Borgnine stomp away. Despite the angry words, to his credit, Cris, the surfer, kept his cool and apologized for the behavior of his father."

Several days later Sylvie told me that she had accompanied Jane Russell to a ladies' function that displayed and promoted beauty products at the Beverly Hills Hotel. Sylvie said, "An attractive lady of about my age greeted us as Tova Borgnine of Beauty by Tova cosmetics. I've always admired successful business people, especially women, so for the sake of civility I forced myself to tell her what a pleasure it was to meet and talk with her husband, Ernest Borgnine. Her look was uninterpretable, and she studied me closely remarking, 'You have good skin. Would you be interested to work for me selling my cosmetics?' I said, 'I manage the Saint John department at Santa Barbara Nordstrom.' She said, 'Oh? Well, please think about it.'

"Right or wrong, there was something discomforting about her, like I was being belittled. I don't know what possessed me to think this and react as I did, and where my perceived notion came from, but nevertheless, as my husband says, *trust your instincts*, which emboldened me to submit myself to a bit of some self-importance. I told her, 'Mr. John Nordstrom came to his store where I work, holding a book my husband had written in 1991, and had sent him an autographed copy. Mr. Nordstrom said the book, *Handbook of Business Quotations*, is very good and he wanted to relay his thanks to my husband. Then he praised me personally, saying that I was the only sales person that received an income equal to that of the general manager's pay because of my many sales commissions.' Voila! Pleased, I managed a smile for Madame Borgnine the cosmetics lady who seemed perplexed, as though she hadn't heard a word I said. She said, 'I wish you would think about it.' I did, and I declined."

# About Actors

Whenever the subject of actors comes up, a frequent response is, "Ah, they're just like the rest of us." This calls to my mind the verbal exchange between F. Scott Fitzgerald and Ernest Hemingway.

Fitz: "The very rich are different from you and me."

Hem: "Yes, they have more money."

About actors:

"The very best actors are different from you and me."

"Yes, they have more celebrity status."

My humble opinion is the best actors are indeed different from us, and these celebrities do know they are different from you and me, because we prove it to them by reading and talking about them and seeing them on the big screen. And they love it. No matter what is said or shown about them—whether it's good, bad, or indifferent—their need is to be talked about. The longevity of their careers depends upon it.

As the nextdoor neighbor and best friend of Jane Russell, my wife Sylvie had many opportunities to become acquainted with a lot of celebrity actors. I asked her what she thought about the topic.

Sylvie: "Just like all of us, some actors are very different, and others are not so different." She added, "Then of course you have male actors and female actors and child actors, and old people who act, so how can you generalize? And broader implications are noteworthy too."

I'm thinking, why must my darling wife at times be so French and overanalyze everything? I can see she knows what I'm thinking. Sylvie says, "Okay, if it will help, what I can tell you is only my own personal experiences with actors whom I am acquainted. Well, let's see… Where to start? Here's an example, and yes, I know I'm to tell you in some sort of formulized story form…to do your work for you." She gives me that familiar smug, teasing half-smile I know so well. And I love her for it, because Sylvie always delivers.

Sylvie: "One sunny morning a big black limousine arrived at Jane Russell's house to take Jane and you  and me to the town of Ojai to pick up the actress June Allyson and her doctor husband to drive the five of us to a Hollywood event in Los Angeles. En route June Allyson said she liked the white outfit I was wearing and asked where I got it. I said, 'It's a Saint John. I manage the Saint John department at the Santa Barbra Nordstrom.' Curiously, she inquired about my working schedule. I assumed that she might visit me there and perhaps make a purchase. I told her, 'Sometimes schedules change, but I am never there on Mondays.' When I arrived for work Tuesday,  my colleague told me excitedly that June Allyson had bought a white outfit Monday that she saw me wearing, consisting of pants, tank top, and cardigan. My colleague was informed a few days later that her commission for the white outfit had been canceled because the client had returned the outfit at another Nordstrom store.

"I learned that it's not uncommon for an item purchased at one store is returned to another store of the same name. Women celebrities often do this, I surmise, in order to stand out in that unique new expensive outfit—for just one occasion."

Chuck: "A good friend of June Allyson visited Jane Russell, and Sylvie and I were invited, among others, to meet Esther Williams, aka America's mermaid. Williams spoke of her deep friendship with June and Jane and how much religion is important to the three of them and how sorry she was that June was unable to be there because the three of them had so much in common. I tried to digest the commonality of her with the Jane Russell I knew, when Williams started using curse words to dramatize whatever point she was trying to make. Startled at the raw language spoken so nonchalantly, Sylvie slinked away. I stood back, struggling to comprehend this former beautifully shaped, athletic swimmer-actress now seated with her obese body squeezed awkwardly into the chair. What happened to America's mermaid? Thyroid? Food addiction, couch potato, no exercise? Maybe she just gave up and said the heck with it. Or, having witnessed her evening's performance as I did, I imagined Miss Williams probably would say, "Who the blank cares. Screw 'em. I'm Esther Williams. And they're not!"

Sylvie said. "Now that's rather harsh, is it not?"

"She's the actor," I responded. "I didn't write her script. She did."

Later I asked Sylvie, "Please tell me of another actor acquaintance of yours?"

Sylvie smiled. Hopefully, I thought, this is a sign of a fetching yarn to come. She took a deep breath and began. "While in Las Vegas with Jane Russell, she took me to see her friend inside the hotel casino. Debbie Reynolds rushed to Jane and they hugged. Jane introduced me, and I knew right away I would like Miss Reynolds (call me Debbie) from the very beginning. She was so gracious and open with a genuine naturalness about her. Debbie gave us the tour of her hotel casino, and the three of us enjoyed a delightful several hours together. Before departing Debbie promised Jane she would come to Santa Barbara, 'one of these days.' When she did arrive, Jane called me. 'Come now. Debbie's here.' That's the way Jane spoke to me, like a big sister. At first I didn't like the curtness, and then I began to love it because that's the way sisters talk to each other, although I never did speak abruptly to Jane. She had her ways, and I have mine, and we had a mutual love for each other, and that's called true friendship. Debbie was as pleasant and perky as ever, and after a chummy visit I excused myself to let America's sweetheart and Hollywood's sex symbol, two compatible acting-dancing-singing pros of the Golden Age of Hollywood, do their own thing. Thinking about these two accomplished film stars who are like us in so many ways, I realized they are also different from us. People like you and me may have our so-called fifteen minutes of fame, while these two multi-talented entertainers remain recognizably famous throughout most of the civilized world by the spellbinding attraction of their movies."

Another time and another call from Jane Russell for Sylvie and me to join them and meet some friends. The very attractive lady and handsome gentleman were introduced to us as Marc and Arlene Rosen. As the evening progressed, conversation disclosed that Marc owned a company that designed perfume bottles and Arlene was an actress during the 40s and 50s. This revelation that she was the film actress Arlene Dahl flashed me back to when my high school girlfriend dragged me to a musical movie against my wishes. The movie was *Three Little Words*. As I recall, a skinny man (Fred Astair) danced, a guy who talked funny (Red Skelton) joked, and a pretty little young girl (Debbie Reynolds) sang. When Arlene Dahl appeared on the screen—the classiest and most glamorous women I'd ever seen—the movie took on a whole new interest. I told my pals about her, and some heckled me, but the curious few that did see the movie (with their girlfriends as a cover) agreed with me about the excitingly sexy, classy, glamorous Arlene Dahl. And here I was now in the home of Jane Russell seated next to my teenage fantasy! Aging had been kind with Arlene, still lovely with an impressive and dignified appearance, married to handsome Marc, her sixth husband and eighteen years younger, and in the year of 1984 when they married, it is said this historical event established Arlene Dahl as the first cougar.

One evening, sitting quietly alone on our patio, Sylvie said, "I have another one for you."

My mind being elsewhere, I asked, "Another what?"

"About another actor. But it's very brief."

"Brevity is the soul of wit."

"What?"

"Never mind. It just came to me."

"Why?"

"Is it a witty story?"

Sylvie said, "I'll tell it my way, then you can do your writer thing with it later." Sylvie began, "Remember that time when Jane and I went to Las Vegas? Well, in the hotel lobby she introduced me to Eva Gabor. When Jane went to the powder room Eva said to me, 'You are pretty. Do you have any sisters?'"

"Yes I do. Four. Dora, Lily, Marie, and Michele."

"Do they look like you?"

"Two of them have a close resemblance."

"Eva said, "Then you and I both have two sisters with similar good looks, and we are both Europeans. I am Hungarian, and you I assume by your accent are French." I nodded, and noted that Eva not only speaks with a pleasing voice, but with expressive eyes as well. Very compelling. I must remember that.

We talked about our accents of Hungarian and French, and Eva asked, "Do you find that because of your accent you gain out of that?"

I nodded. "At times, yes that's so."

And we talked about sisters. Eva said, "One sister of mine is very dominant, as you may know."

I responded with a silent smile to Eva's undisguised reference to her older sister, Zsa Zsa. As kind and friendly as Eva was toward me, I purposely avoid other peoples' family issues, especially matters concerning competitive sisters.

"Voila!" Sylvie said to me. "That's it, my brief story."

Referencing my Shakespeare quote, 'Brevity is the soul of wit,' Sylvie wittily out Shake-speared me with her own improvisation: "To wit or not to wit, that is the question."

I admired her wit with a smile. "Touche, my love."

# A Pleasing Chance Encounter

A tall black man walked toward us across the lobby of a theater in Hollywood. Jane Russell, with her husband John, Sylvie, and I watched him as he approached, singing in a calm, resonate voice. The song was a refrain from "Tall Man" in the film *The Tall Men* starring Jane Russell, Clark Gable, and Robert Ryan. Of course we all knew the man from his films and narrations, and we greeted Morgan Freeman with polite applause.

Morgan Freeman said to Jane, "You know, Miss Russell, I've been waiting a long time for an opportunity to do that."

We all laughed, and Jane said, "Thank you, Mr. Freeman. That was very nice."

"Morgan. Please call me Morgan," he said, and turned his head toward a lady approaching with children. "My wife and kids," he said, and waved them to us. Introductions were made and pleasantries exchanged, followed by a fond farewell. A very pleasing chance meeting indeed!

# A Memorable, Surprising Evening

One autumn evening, Sylvie and I were discussing whether to eat in or go out when the phone rang. Jane Russell was on the line. She said that Stuart Whitman and Martha Smilgis were there with another couple, and for us to come and join them. "Wear sweaters," Jane said. "It's a bit cool out and were eating on the patio." I started to slip into my favorite well-worn, most comfortable sweater when Sylvie shook her head and handed me the new white sweater she had just bought for me at Nordstrom. Having learned not to argue with my wife about food or clothes, I obligingly slipped on the new white sweater and we walked next door to join our friends John and Jane and meet the new couple.

The couple was introduced to us as Bob and Elizabeth Kane. We sat at a round table on the patio overlooking Toro Canyon Creek. John's lamb-and-beef kebab was tasty and fitting for an outdoor evening of casual togetherness. The cool weather was refreshing, and the food and drink contributed to a gay mood of conviviality. I happened to be seated next to Bob, who was an interesting and fun guy. Stuart and his companion, Martha Smilgis, noted author and journalist, were chatting with Elizabeth Kane about the stage play *Country Girl*, in which Elizabeth and Stuart would soon be costarring at a theater in Los Angeles.

This revelation led to the plan that we would all attend the play to see Stuart and Elizabeth perform on stage. Before the evening broke up, Bob touched my shoulder and asked me to turn in my seat. An odd request, I thought, but we had befriended, so I turned. Immediately I felt movement of an object tracing across my back. I glanced at Sylvie, who smiled, indicating approval. As it turned out, the movement was a felt pen drawing of an autographed picture of Batman on my new white sweater, and the artist was Bob Kane, the creator of Batman.

Yes, Bob, I do appreciate this personalized prized possession, which I will cherish, and gives me the freedom to wear my comfortable old sweater—until Sylvie buys me another new one.

# A Lunch Party
# For Friends

One bright day in the month of May, Sylvie declared she had a plan. She decided that the Cliff House Inn at Mussel Shoals Beach a few miles down the coast from Santa Barbara was the ideal spot to host a lunch party in honor of our good friends and neighbors, John and Jane Russell Peoples. Sylvie took the initiative to invite local people whom we had met mostly through John and Jane. In preparation for the event, Sylvie had ordered white cotton t-shirts of varying sizes printed with an image of the two identified as *Big John* and *Bad Jane*, which were handed out to the guests. Among the two dozen close-knit friends who were able to attend the lunch party included actor Stuart Whitman and author-journalist Martha Smilgis, Robert and Dorothy Mitchum, and Andy and Dolly Granatelli. Sylvie also asked a dear French friend to join us. Liliane was the wife of an acclaimed Egyptologist and family heir to the Ricard Pernod S.A. The Ricards lived between homes in France and Santa Barbara, and the engaging couple fit in very well with the other guests.

To condense and sum up the accolades received from the guests, they thanked Sylvie and me for a weather-perfect California day of dining fittingly under a soft sun and mild ocean breeze overlooking the calm sea at an ideal picture-postcard milieu enjoying an abundance of ambiance, comradery, and good cheer with compatible friends.

This occasion happened on the day of my unannounced sixty-second birthday. I gave a wide smile to my cleaver, creative, resourceful wife with a kiss. "Thank you sweetheart, I could never have imagined a better birthday gift."

Major events happened around this time. Sylvie and I moved from Santa Barbara to north central Florida to be near her two sisters, Marie and Michele. Jane Russell's husband, John died of a heart attack. Jane sold her Santa Barbara house and purchased a house seventy miles north in Santa Maria to be near her son, Buck, and daughter-in-law, Etta.

# The Intervention

Several weeks later Buck called me in Florida to report that his mother is with family members who are gathered to convince Jane to go into rehab for her alcoholism, which she steadfastly refuses to do. Buck wanted Sylvie to bring her special relationship of trust and influence with his mother to convince her to go into rehab. Buck said, "A paid round-trip ticket is waiting for Sylvie at Southwest Airlines at the Tampa airport. Please ask Sylvie to come ASAP." Even on such short notice, Sylvie did not hesitate for her best friend, Jane.

Sylvie: "When I arrived at Santa Maria Airport I took a taxi directly to the hospital, where Buck waited for me in the lobby. He took me to the room where family members had gathered around Jane. Jane was happy to see me, and we kissed, then she regarded me despairingly. 'They don't understand,' Jane said. 'I've been to these rehabs before. They just don't work for me. It's a waste of time and money.'

"I said, 'You know, Jane, In France now they have a way to determine if a person is allergic to alcohol.' Jane's eyes widened. 'Allergic!' she exclaimed in a eureka moment. 'That's it. I'm allergic to alcohol!' Her jaw tightened. Angered, she said, 'Why didn't the doctors tell me? I don't need their rehabilitation. I need to stop drinking alcohol because I'm allergic to it.' Regarding me earnestly, she asked, 'What do you think I should do?'

"I was thinking of the family members who had come from different parts of the country in firm determination with the best of intentions to convince Jane to do the rehab. And I thought of my own position in accepting to come for that singular purpose. If Jane started drinking again, the fault would fall on me, which would fracture our friendship. I squeezed her hand. 'Please go to rehab. Discuss the allergy aspect with the doctors.  By doing so, you will please your children and show them that you appreciate their concern for you. You do know I only want the best for you. Under the circumstance I think you should do the rehab. Because if you don't, of course, we'll always be friends, and this is very hard for me to say, but if you refuse and then have a relapse and start drinking again, I would never forgive myself. And I know that would damage our friendship.'

"Jane's eyes locked on me, and I didn't know what to expect. Her head gradually moved side to side, and in feigned exasperation, as only Jane Russell can do, she said, 'There's only one Sylvie.'" Jane spread her arms. 'Come here, kiddo. Come hug Bad Jane.'"

Chuck: "Jane did complete rehabilitation, but not without giving all kinds of hell to the doctors for not telling her that she was allergic to alcohol. Jane Russell, former alcoholic, did not take another alcoholic drink since then. Even after Sylvie and I moved to Florida to be near Sylvie's two sisters, Jane and Sylvie exchanged periodic visits back and forth between Florida and California."

During one of Jane Russell's visits to our home in Florida, she asked, "How far is it to Clearwater from here?"

I said, "Not much over an hour's drive."

"You both know Connie Haines from her visit with me in California," Jane said. "Connie lives in Clearwater. Why not we all go to visit her."

"Great," Sylvie and I agreed. "That'll bring back good times we all had together in Santa Barbara."

Connie's condo lay on a section of sandy beach in Clearwater. When we arrived, Connie introduced us to her dog, Stormy, with equal importance as though the dog was a human. Tiny, feisty, rascal Stormy proved to be appropriately named from one of Connie's popular songs "Stormy Weather."

Right away, Connie remarked to Jane, "What did you do to your eyes? They were much better before."

Jane responded in kind, "I see you're sporting a scarf. Turkey-neck issues?"

With this exchange of playful barbs, speaking only as sisters and tight friends do, they launched into a buddy-buddy reminiscence of good times when they joined with English singer Beryl Davis. The three ladies put on an act singing spirituals in night clubs, of all places—and with success. Connie and Jane chuckled about the critic who called their act 'Bosoms and Bibles.' They loved it, and so did their fans. Connie was the most accomplished singer of the trio, having teamed with Frank Sinatra in Tommy Dorsey's band, and awarded top female singer with Harry James's big band.

Connie, nee Yvone Marie Antoinette, being of French ancestry, shared an affinity with Sylvie. They shared fun stories about the times they had together with Jane in Santa Barbara. With their comradeship reawakened, they decided that Connie should visit us at our Florida home. Connie did come, and we had a wonderful visit with only one snag. With Connie's approval Sylvie asked the retired widows, whose club's primary purpose was to meet available men, if the famous singer, widow Connie Haines, could join them among the men. The immediate reply from the highly competitive not-so-merry widows was a resounding, "No!"

Too soon, our friend, devout Christian and spiritual song-stress, died at age 87 on September 22, 2009, survived by Connie's incredible 109-year-old mother. Loss of a friend is a sorrowful matter, yet with her unrelenting faith we knew Connie Haines most assuredly will be singing spirituals in eternal peace.

# Jane Russell's Last Visit To Florisa

One January day in 2011, Jane Russell called us from California that she accepted a singing gig in Palm Beach, and she gave us the dates since she planned to stay with us a couple of weeks in Florida before returning to California. "Perfect," Sylvie said. "Our niece, Theresa, is getting married here at the Ocala Hilton during your stay. Would like to join us?" Jane said," Of course, honey, you go I go."

Chuck: When I picked Jane up at Tampa Airport, I could see right away she was not well. The drive to our home was slow because Jane needed frequent rest stops. When we got to our house, Sylvie had left a note saying she was staying overnight at the Hilton Hotel with Theresa's mother, Marie, where they were supervising wedding arrangements. Once I got Jane comfortably settled into the guest bedroom, I went directly to bed. In the middle of the night I heard sounds coming from the kitchen. Jane was in her night gown looking lost. I said, "What do you need, Jane?" She turned to me with a confused, helpless look and muttered, "I can't breathe."

Responding to my 911 call, the emergency medical vehicle arrived within minutes. Surrounding the many retirement communities in north-central Florida, to avoid the press, I told the driver to take her to Seven Rivers Hospital in Crystal River, a competent discreet hospital I knew of near the Gulf. I followed the ambulance and checked Jane in under her married name, Jane Peoples.

Sylvie and I attended our niece's wedding that evening, and we went to the hospital early the next day. After a brief visit I departed, and Sylvie dug in for what turned out to be a month-long stay with Jane. Sylvie explained to me that she slept lightly in a reclining armchair in the single room with Jane. One night she was awakened by a movement in the room. Feigning to be asleep, she watched a male nurse step to Jane's bedside. He began to pray, "Dear Lord, take this daughter and not to let her suffer any more." And he continued to pray, and Sylvie was touched by this nurse's spiritual words for a suffering patient in pain. His arm moved, and Sylvie saw him slide the syringe into his pocket without having given the pain abating injection. How odd she thought, dozing off, until she heard a shrill scream and saw Jane standing at bedside with tears running down her cheeks. Sylvie sprang from the chair, sounded the alarm, and rushed to the door calling for help. Sylvie explained the syringe incident to a nurse, who said the male nurse posted that he had given the injection. Sylvie insisted before a higher authority that the male nurse did not give Jane the injection, and she signed a formal statement declaring such, which resulted in the firing of the cruel profiteering, thieving, lying male nurse.

When Jane was released after a month from the hospital, her son, Buck, arranged for an ambulance flight from Ocala, Florida to Santa Maria, California. Jane insisted that Sylvie accompany her all the way and remain with her at her home. Sylvie did as her loving friend insisted, and she and Jane's daughter, Tracy, stayed at Jane's bedside until Jane passed away on February 28, 2011, age 89.

Chuck: Terry Moore called me daily about Jane's failing condition, until I heard of Jane's death directly from Terry herself.

She said Jane and she were very close, and that Jane was Howard Hughes's star, and that she, Terry, was Hughes's wife. On one such call when the subject of the ambulance plane came up about flying Jane back to California from Florida, Terry said that if she had known she would have called her dear friend John Travolta to fly Jane back home in his own airplane. Travolta resided at Jumbolair Aviation Estates with his wife Kelly Preston, and his Boeing 707. This private, gated aviation community with two long airstrips was situated about twenty-five miles from our home in the same county in north-central Florida. At Jane's Celebration of Life ceremony, Terry sought out Sylvie to tell her that Jane had told her about so many nice things Sylvie had done for her, and how appreciative Jane was for having such a good, helpful friend as Sylvie.

# Epilogue: A Close-Up of Jane Russell

Much has been said and written about Jane Russell and her relationships, especially those of iconic celebs Robert Mitchum, Howard Hughes, Marilyn Monroe, Bob Hope…and Jane's breasts. For two decades Sylvie and Jane shared much of their own personal backgrounds. Here are some of Jane's experiences she told to Sylvie.

Robert Mitchum and Jane Russell's relationship grew out of the two movies in which they co-starred, *His Kind of Woman* and *Macao*, out of which developed a full-fledged affair between them until Robert Mitchum's wife, Dorothy, spoke to Jane about it. Knowing Jane was very religious, Dorothy appealed to Jane's Christian beliefs in a calm, mature manner, for the Lord's sake to please stop the affair. Jane and Robert did stop their trysts, and all persons affected by the affair remained close friends.

Jane and Robert and their all-knowing respective spouses, John Peoples and Dorothy Mitchum, remained tight-knit couples, and the foursome continued together around the social circuit, and all the while Jane kept Robert Mitchum's love notes and poems secreted inside her piano bench, and 'His Kind of Woman,' Robert Mitchum kept sending Jane more love poems. Hooray for Hollywood!

It's hard to think of Jane Russell and Marilyn Monroe without picturing these two bankable stars together in the universally popular musical comedy *Gentlemen Prefer Blonds*. Casting these two sex symbols in the same comic movie was pure Hollywood genius. And according to Jane, the playful banter they exhibited on screen overlapped into real life. Marilyn says she likes to feel blond all over, after which Jane calls her *Blondel*. On Marilyn's serious side, she told Jane she was not one to abide by all the rules, and she will do whatever it takes to succeed in this business. At times insecure and often late for work, Marilyn was dedicated to the immediate job at hand, and she was sweet with cast and crew. Once Jane, a very religious person, invited Marilyn to a prayer gathering of a group of Jane's relatives and like friends. Afterward, Marilyn politely thanked Jane but said it was just not for her. Jane said the two of them got along well together professionally and socially, and neither spoke negatively of the other. *Gentlemen Prefer Blonds* was one of those Hollywood unions crying out for another Russell Monroe blockbuster, which regrettably never happened.

Hollywood film tycoon Howard Hughes chose Jane Russell among many girls auditioning for the part of Rio in Hughes' film *The Outlaw*. Jane always spoke publicly of Howard being a quiet, shy man, and always a gentleman, and Howard had made only one sexual attempt with her. One evening in 1947, around the time of Jane's pending divorce with Robert Waterfield, at Hughes's Bel Air house, she and Howard were discussing Jane's new contract conditions, and the hours passed so it was decided it was too late for Jane to drive home alone. Jane's public story is that she stayed over, and during the night she heard a sound and looked up. Standing at her bedside, Howard said he was cold and could he join her. Jane confessed she agreed, but when Howard started to make his moves she repelled his advances. Jane dozed off and awoke in the morning alone. Howard was gone, so she drove home without a further word about it.

In spite of Jane's public insistence that her relationship with Howard was friendly, platonic, and business-related only, gossip persisted of sexual dalliances supported by the argument, why else would Hughes have given Jane a one-thousand dollar a week twenty-year contract? When this subject came up privately with Sylvie, Jane told her, "Howard was loyal, and as good as his word. A darling man, and I loved him." Jane told Sylvie that she did have "romantic encounters" with Howard, but didn't elaborate further—and a lady doesn't pry.

After Jane's death at her Santa Maria home, Sylvie overheard Jane's sons, Thomas and Buck, wondering aloud if their mother had sex with Howard Hughes. Their sister, Tracy, chimed in saying that one day she was out with her mother when the car stopped at Howard Hughes's house. Her mother said she'd be back shortly. Tracy and the chauffer waited until her mom finally reentered the car, with her hair messed up.

Bob Hope and Jane Russell costarred in two well received comedy films, *The Paleface* and *Son of Paleface*. At an overseas USO event, Hope introduced Jane to the troops as "The two and only Jane Russell." This obvious reference to her well-endowed assets won howls and whistles of approval. And when Jane replied, "Bob calls me Lumpy," the noise volume doubled. It was well known around the Hollywood scene of who's sleeping with who that Bob Hope was a womanizer and he had sexual affaires with most, if not all his leading ladies, including Jane Russell.

Sylvie and I happened to be in California visiting Jane when a camera crew arrived to Jane's Santa Maria home in late July 2003 for a Larry King telephone interview with Jane about Bob Hope (who died July 27, 2003 at age 100). Much was bantered about Bob and Jane, their comic movies and close friendship, and under King's questioning Jane said of her leading men, "Bob Hope was the best kisser of them all."

A note about Bob Hope's remark, "The two and only Jane Russell" —Sylvie was told by both Jane and Jane's long-time very close friend, Babs Allen, that the two of them had met and bonded in a sanitarium—Jane for alcoholism and Babs for nervous breakdown. After their releases from the asylum, Babs, a former swimsuit model, agreed to be the front to buy Jane's bras because of Howard Hughes's obsession with large breasts, which he mega-promoted in his first movie, *The Outlaw*, starring Jane Russell. If the famous movie star sex symbol, whose breast size is actually proportionally normal, was seen buying smaller size bras other than advertised, the secret would be out. The myth continues.

# A Special Place In Time

After Jane died neither Sylvie nor I returned to Santa Maria. However, I did fly out from Florida a couple of times to visit with my pal Stuart Whitman in Santa Barbara. Those trips sadly faded, but not the impressionable memories of Santa Barbara in the 1990s. A rare and veritable moveable feast indeed.

www.ingramcontent.com/pod-product-compliance
Lightning Source LLC
LaVergne TN
LVHW021543080426
835509LV00019B/2816